Virginia

Virginia

A Play
by
Edna O'Brien

Revised Edition

A Harvest/HBJ Book
Harcourt Brace Jovanovich, Publishers
San Diego   New York   London

Library of Congress Cataloging in Publication Data

O'Brien, Edna.
Virginia: a play.

1. Woolf, Virginia, 1882-1941, in fiction, drama, poetry, etc.
I. Title.
PR6065.B7V5   822'.914   81-7663
ISBN 0-15-193762-1
ISBN 0-15-693560-0 (Harvest/HBJ : pbk.)

Printed in the United States of America

First Harvest/HBJ edition, 1985

A B C D E F G H I J

TO

Nigel Nicolson

First performed in June 1980 by the Stratford Shakespearean Festival Foundation of Canada at the Avon Theatre, Stratford, Ontario, by arrangement with H. M. Tennent Ltd and subsequently presented in London in January 1981 by H. M. Tennent Ltd at the Theatre Royal, Haymarket.

This edition was prepared from the revised script for Joseph Papp's New York Shakespeare Festival production in 1985.

The Characters

VIRGINIA appears as a grown woman and also as her youthful self. Her mode of talking varies drastically. She is at times quick, high-spirited; other times ruminative, and once like a somnambulist. She talks to THE MAN, to herself, and to the audience and when she is talking her "writing," it is in another vein altogether—reflective, rapturous, dreamlike.

THE MAN appears first as an old man—her father. He wears a greatcoat and in his several pockets there is a book. He always has a book to hand and is often seen to be muttering under his breath. The mutter is inaudible, it is this:
  "But I beneath a rougher sea
  Was whelmed in deeper gulf."

Next he is LEONARD WOOLF. There is a notable contrast in his first appearance as LEONARD, when he strides in, full of vigor, like any young man about to propose to any young woman. In later scenes he has a pronounced tremor.

VITA appears as a dashing woman of 37, regal bearing, with bohemian manners. She is sensuality as opposed to VIRGINIA'S etherealness.

Virginia

Act One

Scene One

VIRGINIA:
I dreamt that I leant over the edge of the boat and fell down. I went under the sea; I have been dead and yet am now alive again—it was awful, awful, and as before waking, the voices of the birds and the sound of wheels chime and chatter in a queer harmony, grow louder and louder and the sleeper feels himself drawing towards the shores of life, the sun growing hotter, cries sounding louder, something tremendous about to happen.

MAN:
Ginny—Virginia—

[VIRGINIA *looks at him.*]

VIRGINIA:
Moments, moments of my being . . . in here, captive. My father bent over his tomes . . . no light lover he, no superficial optimist, one of the giant breed, alone in the ice-bound seas.

My two bloods dashing together. My father's scrutinous, bold, brutal, an oarsman, coach of oarsmen. And my mother's decorous, beautiful and afraid.

His wife my mother. When she was presiding it was all very moving and very stirring, the room full of people, her several children, the nursery ceiling very high and plates and plates of innocent bread and butter.

Life and a little strip of time presented itself to her eyes, to her fifty years. She took a look at life, and she had a clear sense of it, something real, something private which she shared with neither her children nor her husband. She was always trying to get the better of it, as it was of her, and sometimes they parleyed; she felt this thing called Life terrible, hostile and quick to pounce on you. And then she said, brandishing her sword, "Nonsense."

Yes I wanted her to myself; one does. I wanted to be singled out. I would show her my little stories about souls flying about looking for bodies. She liked that. My mother, his wife, not at all the same thing. It must be a strange thing to be man and wife, all that copulation. Marriage and motherhood without awakenment. It is not enough. Rather crowded and rather anxious and very valiant but it is not enough. Her pride in him was like the pride of one in some lofty mountain peak visited only by the light of the stars, noble, yes, enthusiastic, yes, but humble, too humble. My mother. One says it. One cannot not say it. A single phrase, or her voice, or that beautiful figure so upright in the ground, in her long shabby cloak, the head held high, so upright and so distinct and the eyes that looked straight ahead, hurrying, saying,

"Come along, quick, quick; don't keep Father waiting."

Or sitting there writing a letter at the table, and the silver candle-sticks and the high carved chair and the three-cornered brass ink-pot and then not there.

She was upstairs and my half-brother George Duckworth took me into her bedroom to kiss her good-bye and she said, "Hold yourself straight, my little goat." It was May the fifth, eighteen-ninety-five.

It was about six in the morning. I saw the doctor walk away, I saw the pigeons floating, settling.

They wrapped towels around me and gave me brandy; I think the sun was coming up. She had just died.

Death plays havoc.

MAN:
No, no, no.

VIRGINIA [*resistant*]:
Shut up.

Scene Two

VIRGINIA:
We rallied, my sister and I, we rallied. That was the thing. That was the supreme test. My father, bent, unstrung, saying the same thing over and over again.

MAN:
I never told her I never told her how much I loved her.

[*Repeated several times*]

VIRGINIA:
The house was full of mourners, women, pathos, bathos.

The black-edged border so thick that there was no room for the message. He had not told her that he loved her. The old story. Too late.

MAN:
I was not as bad as Carlyle, was I?

VIRGINIA:
He wants comfort but what comfort can we give?

MAN:
Everyone has forgotten me.

VIRGINIA:
A skinless man and skinless children.

Let him be fifty feet away, let him not even speak, not even see you, he permeated, he prevailed, he demanded; one pretended to drink from a cup to escape his demands, to put aside a moment longer that imperious need. . . . Do this, do that . . . his dominance, his "Submit to me."

The words wrote themselves, leaf upon leaf, fold upon fold, incessant, upon the brain.

For no one attracted me more; his hands were beautiful to me and his feet, and his voice and his words, and his haste and his temper and his oddity and his passion, and his saying straight out before everyone:

MAN:
"We perish each alone."

VIRGINIA:
And his remoteness.

MAN:
What did you say?

VIRGINIA:
Crushed and cranked in the womb by your important works and now having to be grown up and tell you that you are not as bad as Mr. Carlyle. So selfish, such inconceivable selfishness.

Hate rising up in me against him, sharpening, sharpening.

So selfish and so stingy. When my sister Nessa asked for the housekeeping money he said she should be ashamed of herself and that she would make us bankrupt. No wonder I had tantrums *and* fidgets.

Along with that, my sister and I had to come out. To come out on nothing. That silly world of white satin and kid gloves and visiting cards and young men from the Foreign Office who never heard of Plato but who could dance.

The man or the woman who shines at a dance is at the center of things. Lord Gayton and Nancy Blowe—they met, they danced and that was it. So clear, so clever, such enormous resources.

MAN:

To be them would be marvelous but she is condemned to be herself. By some malice of fate she is unable to join in.

VIRGINIA:

Eros came on dirty wings. My half-brother George was taking me to Lady Sligo's Ball.

My dress was made of green stuff bought at a furniture shop because it was cheaper and also more adventurous. The carriage waiting, the pavement silver in the new moon, half insane with shyness and with nervousness, I entered the Ball. . . . And gallopaded around the room discussing oratory and the Garter with young men from the Foreign Office. Dancing, feeling the queerness and the strangeness of being alone with a complete stranger, striking out this way and that like a beginner on ice. My half-brother George danced with all the ladies and then bowed to them, then brought me home.

I went up to my bedroom, unfastened the brooch that he gave me and then: the door opened and in the dark someone entered— "Who?" I cried. "Don't be frightened," George replied, "and don't turn on the light, oh beloved."

He flung himself on my bed and took me in his arms. Something in him burst, reticence, you could say, or decency or etiquette, the things that middle-class men are supposed to possess. "Besides, I love you, I must have you," he said.

The division in our lives was most curious. There was my father in the next room teaching me the humanities and the sciences, the rules against error. All theory, vapid, theory.

I am unlearned. Make no mistake, the Greeks are for men, the Treasury is for men, Whitehall is for men, the world belongs to men.

[*She looks at* THE MAN.]

I wanted a mind, a man, a sparring partner, but they were all in Cambridge. My brother Thoby was in Cambridge.

If the spirit of peace dwelt anywhere it was in those rooms in Cambridge, those courts, those quadrangles, colors burning in the windowpane like the beat of an excitable heart . . . all the books and smoke and drink and deep armchairs . . . the urbanity.

The dignity.

MAN:
The privacy.

VIRGINIA [*ignoring him*]:
My brother Thoby knew the most interesting fellows, apostles and geniuses.

[*Very excited*]

Lytton Strachey a wit, Sydney Turner another, slept all day and read all night; Woolf a strange wild man, a Jew; Clive Bell an atheist and what is more a muscular atheist, who not only wrote poems but had Edna May to lunch in his rooms, dammit, while we famished at home and tackled Greek and did bookbinding and laid the table and were polite to women, to Aunts, women in constant lachrymose attendance for every death and every deathknock.

MAN:
Ginia, you are such a comfort to me, so good to me.

VIRGINIA:
If you must die, why don't you?

[VIRGINIA *turns as if she is about to recall him but doesn't. She crosses and snaps closed the book that he was reading.*]

VIRGINIA:
His life would have entirely ended mine—no writing, no rooks slicing the air, no stories, inconceivable.

It was a question of throwing out all the old things, the stacks of letters, the pictures, the Past, and moving to Gordon Square. It was a most beautiful thing to have distempered walls and bright chintzes, to have coffee instead of tea.

And Nessa and I no longer in white satin but in colored dresses like Gauguin painted.

And so began our Thursdays. The bell would ring after dinner and in they glided, Strachey and Sydney Turner and Leonard Woolf and Clive Bell. Clive Bell, a mixture between Shelley and a country squire. Lytton Strachey.

[*Ponderous voice*] "Do you hear the music of the spheres," and then fainting; and Sydney Turner, who only spoke the truth, the absolute truth.

And I had to hide the matchboxes because they clashed with the colors.

They would settle themselves in corners and gaze into the distance and for a long time say nothing.

"No,"

"No, I have not seen it,"

"No, I have not been there,"

"No, I do not agree."

Until they got on to something really interesting such as beauty or whether intimacy led to a dust of the soul.

Every word had an aura. Poetry combined the different auras in a sequence.

I would think I am a story, he is a story, she is a story, but how to get it. Not just the theory and the argument, holding the thing —all the things—the innumerable things together. Phrases for the moon, how people looked, turned, dropped their cigarette ends. And then Strachey, who hadn't spoken for ages, suddenly pointed to a stain on Nessa's skirt and said "Semen?" Can one really say it, I thought. And suddenly we were all laughing. Nessa laughed the most. How beautiful she was and how ready.

She was the sunlight and I was the twilight. Love was not mentioned. Anyhow the great artist was Androgynous. I had known that there were buggers in Plato's Greece but it never occurred to me that there could be buggers in our drawing room in Forty-six Gordon Square.

James is in despair, Rupert has been twice jilted, Morgan isn't coping.

Marriage was a lowdown affair and yet

[*Reciting*]

"Miss Buss and Mr. Beale
Cupid's darts do feel."

I never dreamed it would happen.

Nessa put her arms above her head and said, "I can see that we shall marry." I could feel the fate that would descend and snatch us apart, we who had been drawn together as though by some capillary attraction, we who had ruled the world between us.

[*Crisply*] "Marry? Who?"

VIRGINIA [*as* NESSA]:
"Whoever."

VIRGINIA [*as herself*]:
"Marry? Our father not long dead and you talk of marry."

Women are hard to women. Women dislike women.

[*To* NESSA] "It's indecent. . . . Marry . . . ? Who?"

VIRGINIA [*as* NESSA]:
"Clive, for instance."

VIRGINIA [*as herself*]:
"He is not good enough. A jerky little man who chases girls. He even discusses modern verse with a jerk."

[*Addressing him*] "You are all sensitive appreciations, Mr. Bell, but you have no character, you lack bottom."

[*To* NESSA] "He blushes like a sunset and blinks like a windmill."

[*To the Audience*] I couldn't stop her; she began to put roses behind her ear and wear the pink cloak that we bought on our travels in Constantinople. She began seeing him every day. I would have to come between them because she was everything to me . . . she was mother, father, brother, sister, lover.

[*Turns away abruptly*]

It was then I hatched my little plan.

To come between them. Jealousy at the bottom of it. Jealousy which survives every other passion of mankind.

Oh Clive, I am so palpitating, I am so affectionate, I cannot write a novel, because I cannot find the right pen, and Clive, if we go for another walk shall I come in woollies?

He was someone to make the afternoons hum. I would rub up his wits and in return get my manners polished. How we talked, a plethora of talk, about the elephants in Kent or potted tongue or Rousseau or whether it was colder in the eighteenth century or why the Russians had no sense of humor. And she would be left at home to mind their baby. I believe he hated that baby . . . as I believe I did . . . he and I had that in common, we hated babies and Nessa loved them. She clapped when it burped.

[*Sarcastically*] And as for babies' wonderful plops and no sign of measles, touch wood. "Clive, what is the origin of touch wood?" And he would take down the encyclopaedia, and one day he said to me, he said, "Virginia, what is the brightest thing you can think of?" And I said, "A leaf with a light on it," and I meant it. She saw us go arm in arm across the downs. Then one day she called me aside—it was after the three of us had been to Florence—and she was so kind about it, but that was because she was hurt. She said, "Now, Virginia, we know it's not true, we all know that it's not true, but your Aunts would say that you are flirting with my husband." And then she said, "If you had loved him, I would not mind so much, but you do not love him."

[VIRGINIA *flounces away as if from her sister and is haughty.*]

VIRGINIA:
Love, there is something faintly ridiculous about it.

[*Reciting*]

"How different from us,
Mr. Beale and Miss Buss."

[*Barrel organ*]

Far preferable to go out into the London street and toss my brain in the air. What a lark, what a plunge, how fresh, how calm the air, June, June that draws out every leaf on every tree. Mothers of Pimlico giving suck to their young.

Messages passing from the Fleet to the Admiralty. Arlington Street and Piccadilly seemed to chaff the very air. . . . London gay and defiant.

Ah, Mr. Woolf. I hear you have done wonders in Ceylon, governing natives, shooting tigers, hanging blacks.

LEONARD:
I'm glad to be home.

VIRGINIA:
Tell me something about Ceylon, something I don't know.

LEONARD:
One day I was traveling by train and there were all those dead sharks on the seashore and they all had this strange smile, this strange smirk.

VIRGINIA [*disbelieving*]:
Really. And what do you do since you came home?

LEONARD:
I cycle about, I see my old friends from Cambridge. . . . I go for walks, I discuss G. E. Moore.

VIRGINIA:
Still?

LEONARD:
I've been to the Zoo. The lions behave as if they had been born in South Kensington.

VIRGINIA:
How, how?

LEONARD:
I saw a curious incident. The lions were in their indoor cages. A stout, middle-aged, middle-class lady was standing near the bars looking at a magnificent lion who was standing on the other side of the bars gazing over her head, as lions seem to do, into eternity. Suddenly he turned round, presented his backside to her and pissed on her through the bars. "Oh, the dirty beast," she said. "Oh, the dirty beast."

VIRGINIA [*laughing*]:
Oh, the dirty beast.

[*She laughs and then suddenly stops.*]

That's a stupid thing; haven't you anything better to say?

LEONARD:
Yes. [*Pause*] Marry me.

VIRGINIA [*aside*]:
Why does everyone talk of marriage—is it crude human nature breaking out?

LEONARD:
It is true that I am cold and reserved to other people.

VIRGINIA:
According to yourself.

LEONARD:
I am selfish, cruel, lustful and a liar.

VIRGINIA:
In a dream you argued so violently that you pulled your own thumb out of joint. You have the temper of Dean Swift and would murder your wife. You would whizz a tea plate through a window.

LEONARD [*quickly*]:
I expect Thoby told you that. [*Lower voice*] I'm sorry he died.

VIRGINIA [*sharply*]:
We don't mention it. We've had too many deaths, my mother, my father, my half-sister, Stella, then Thoby. It's against our code to mourn.

[*She turns her back on him.*]

LEONARD:
I have waited six years for you.

VIRGINIA:
You seem so foreign, so disquietingly foreign.

[*She stamps her foot.*]

No, I won't marry you.

[*To the Audience*] Cruel . . . cru . . . el. I love cruelty. I could eat it on a spoon like malt and oil.

[*She turns round and walks downstage to the Audience.*]

LEONARD [*to Virginia, as if he were writing a letter*]:
My dearest Virginia,
I must write you—I have not got any very clear recollection of what I said to you this afternoon but I am sure you know why I came—I never realized how much I loved you until we talked about my going back to Ceylon. After that I could think about

nothing else but you. I got into a state of hopeless uncertainty, whether you loved me or could ever love me or even like me.

VIRGINIA:
There isn't really anything for me to say except that I should like to go on as before and that you should leave me free.

LEONARD:
Something in you seems to rise up against me.

VIRGINIA:
I pass from hot to cold in an instant and without any reason.

LEONARD:
Apart from being in love with you it would be worth the risk of everything to marry you.

VIRGINIA:
I love other people to have houses, mats, tables, chairs, pictures, china, tapestry over the four-poster bed, lavender in chamber pots and biscuits in a tin, should one waken hungry in the night. Other people in their vile little villas in the suburbs smelling of meat and humanity, all very dull and all very sensible.

[*As an aside*] Besides, I feel no physical attraction for you. There are moments, when you kissed me the other day was one, when I feel no more enraptured than a rock.

LEONARD:
You have danced your marriage away, like Hippokliedes.

VIRGINIA:
Like who?

LEONARD:
Hippokliedes—he got rather above himself.

VIRGINIA [*smiling*]:
Maybe I will marry you.

[LEONARD *turns and sees her smile.*]

VIRGINIA:
I only ask for someone to make me vehement and then I'll marry
them.

LEONARD:
Maybe I will make you vehement.

VIRGINIA:
I've got a disease, you know, in the head. My pulse passes the limits
of reason, goes insane. I walk making up phrases, I sit contriving
scenes. . . .

LEONARD:
Someday you might write something astonishingly good.

VIRGINIA:
And you?

LEONARD:
I will earn my living in Fleet Street and write my masterpieces in
the evening. [*He smiles.*] Newspaper offices are paved with master-
pieces.

VIRGINIA:
We ask a great deal of life, don't we?

LEONARD:
Perhaps we shall get it.

[*Suddenly* VIRGINIA *takes off her mother's ring and gives it to
him.*]

VIRGINIA:
It was my mother's; take it . . . don't ask me why.

LEONARD:
Let's go to St. Pancras. . . .

[*Thunderstorm*]

VIRGINIA [*turns back to Audience*]:
Saved, saved by marriage; what a preposterous thing.

Scene Three

LEONARD:
Whatever hour you woke there was a door shutting. From room to room they went, hand in hand, lifting here, opening there, making sure—a ghostly couple.

[*Clock*]

VIRGINIA [*very rapidly*]:
Eleven o'clock, twelve o'clock, thirteen, fourteen and so on, until they reach twenties and then thirties and then forties and fifties and sixties.

There is nothing to prevent them, phantoms of the foulest kind.

I hate this body . . . this belly . . . it's sordid . . . demand, mouth, food, lust; it's repulsive. What enemy do we now perceive advancing against us?

Let the Jew speak.

To me all teaching and preaching is a blasphemy . . . communists, socialists, Roman Catholics, . . . Fabians—think they can affect the destiny of nations.

If that's for me, you know what to do with it; pooh, pooh, the goat is mad, the goat is not mad. And I am not mad. Mrs. Thackeray is mad. I know for instance that five hundred a year is considerably more valuable than beauty or rank. I am lazy, inane, gluttonous and the treatment is no good. [*Abrasive voice*] I said the treatment is no good.

Committees, committees—committees for babies, committees for lunatics, a committee for the sick, the disabled and the dead.

[*Pointing a finger at him*] You are like one of those mowing machines that go round and round until finally their little square of corn is cut.

[*Laughing*] I have read your diary, I have cracked your code, your Singhalese code, V—good, fair or bad day, good, fair or bad night, as if I was a weathercock.

[*Flauntingly*] There is no gate, no lock, no bolt that you can set upon the freedom of my mind. . . . And for me neither, no gate, no lock, no bolt.

LEONARD:
Just one spoonful, just one.

VIRGINIA:
It's disgusting, it's the entrail of pigs . . . it oozes.

LEONARD:
It's just arrowroot.

VIRGINIA:
To be wise and to be happy. Those are the hardest things.

LEONARD:
You *are* wise and you are happy.

VIRGINIA:
Suddenly how gentle you are. One of your tricks.

Once you fall, human nature is upon you. Human nature is remorseless.

Call the nurse, call the doctor, call the do-gooders. My mother's met them, she's just told me. She said, "Virginia, the dead are very boring and very conventional, just like the living." What a chance the British aristocracy had and lost it. I mean if they'd grafted some brain onto those stupid bodies with their housemaid sensibilities. And tell me, tell me why do people make such a fuss about marriage and copulation. Answer me. Such a stink. We didn't, did we? We saw straight away that it was stupid, nasty, phew.

That woman is laughing at me.

And are you buffeting against the gale, are you?

Get away from me, brute; I know what you want, I know what you all want. One thing, I foretold the murder of the Archduke and the death of Mrs. Robert Louis Stevenson.

[*Forcing herself to be brave*]

Yes, one must meet one's apparitions.

The violets are there and the daffodils.

[*She is now in real terror and like an animal.*]

You will put me away; people like you always do. With your blue books and your good causes, look at him, Mama, the man I married, the puppet. He said, [*turning to* LEONARD] you said,

LEONARD:
There is some primitive valve in our hearts, some primeval cell in our brains, handed down to us from our reptilian, piscine or simian ancestors which makes us peculiarly, primordially sensitive to the mother's death.

VIRGINIA [*hitting him*]:
Thinking you can affect the destiny of nations, you can't do anything for your wife; why am I like this? Because of you . . . yes, I am inchoate. . . .

Don't put me away, please don't put me away. It's so cold, it's so awful, you have no idea, it's so far away. My mother, my mystery. Why am I talking to my mother? It's so cold.

Must muffle up against the night air. Must haul myself into this particular coat that belongs to me. . . . Must, must.

Who are you?

[*Walks downstage into darkness.*]

Scene Four

LEONARD:
It's for your birthday.

VIRGINIA [*timidly*]:
Shall I open it?

[*She opens it and takes out a beautiful green beaded bag with a chain handle. She puts it on her wrist.*]

VIRGINIA:
Wouldn't Lady Dilke love it?

LEONARD:
And you can look now.

[VIRGINIA *turns round and sees the printing press.*]

LEONARD:
It's a printing press. I got it in the Holborn viaduct for nineteen pounds, five shillings and fivepence.

VIRGINIA:
What shall we do with it?

LEONARD:
We shall print and we shall sell by subscription.

VIRGINIA:
What shall we print? The k-aa-te sat on the m-aa-te.

LEONARD:
Come on, try it.

VIRGINIA:
I'm afraid of it.

LEONARD:
It will be good for you, something physical.

VIRGINIA:
I know what I'll print—

There is no casement so magic as ours.

I shall tell you wonderful stories of the lunatics by and by. They elected me king and before I left I summoned a conclave and made a proclamation about Christianity.

I should hate to fail, I should hate to go under again—months, years, wiped out of one's life.

LEONARD:
Here you are thinking, planning, printing, pressing forward, solid.

VIRGINIA:
Let's gallop to it.

The Wise Virgins by Leonard Woolf.

LEONARD:
Kew Gardens by Virginia Woolf.

VIRGINIA:
Prelude by Katherine Mansfield.

LEONARD:
Night and Day by Virginia Woolf.

[*Reciting*]

. . . breaking the silence with such depth of contentment, such passion of desire, or in the voices of children such freshness of surprise breaking the silence.

VIRGINIA:
Will we have children?

LEONARD:
Maybe . . . not.

VIRGINIA:
Oh, Mongoose.

LEONARD:
Oh, Mandrill.

VIRGINIA:
I wrote to you every day.

[*Quoting*] "Precious Mongoose, I lie and think of my special beast who does make me happy every day of my life."

LEONARD:
And I read it every day.

VIRGINIA:
And what else did Mongoose do?

LEONARD:
At the weekends I walked on the downs near Asheham and I could hear the pounding of the guns on the Flanders field. I thought of my poor brothers, Cecil and Philip, Rupert Brooke and all of them. I mind them being in the trenches and I mind being exempt and I hate this blasted shake of mine.

VIRGINIA:
What would I do without you?

LEONARD:
War changes nothing; it's just a costly muddle.

VIRGINIA:
Mister Asquith says we are fighting for the moral forces of humanity. . . .

LEONARD:
Mister Asquith is a fool. And that's hubristic patriotism. Nellie
made a stew.

VIRGINIA:
A nut stew.

LEONARD:
Probably.

VIRGINIA:
I dream with rapture of roast mutton, don't you?

LEONARD:
No, chocolate creams.

VIRGINIA:
Or cold grouse and rough pâté and pineapple chunks.

LEONARD:
On Sunday we could go blackberrying.

VIRGINIA:
When you eat toast you look like a rabbit. . . . Your nose twitches.

Go on . . . eat it.

[*Happily*] A wild rabbit. A king rabbit. A rabbit that makes laws
for all other rabbits.

[*Stretching her arms up*] This is life and I adore it.

Lettuce, Rabbit?

Come and take it out of my hand.

Not a tame rabbit either. Lapin.

LEONARD:
Simply and solely English, desiring melancholy like most English
people.

VIRGINIA:

Lapin . . . lapin . . . king lapin . . . I am always finding new qualities in you, and every day I shall say, "And what did the King do today?"

LEONARD:

"Today," said the King, twitching his nose as he lit his cigar, "today I chased a hare. A woman hare."

VIRGINIA:

A white hare, with big eyes.

LEONARD:

Yes, with eyes popping out of her head.

VIRGINIA:

Aah . . . Lapinova.

LEONARD:

Is that what she's called, Lapinova?

VIRGINIA:

Yes, that's what she's called. She's wary and undependable, whereas he is bold, and determined. They breed like rabbits.

LEONARD:

Little devils. Shoot 'em. Jump on them with bog boots. So says the Squire.

VIRGINIA:

Oh, King Lapin, if you weren't here and if your nose didn't twitch I should be miserable.

[*Telephone rings.*]

LEONARD:

Not at home. Not at home.

[VIRGINIA *goes to answer the phone with a flourish.*]

VIRGINIA:
Ah, the world wants us . . . how splendid. I like to feel important
after writing. . . . Writing quivers you.

[*She picks up the phone.*]

LEONARD:
Say that we're going to the country.

VIRGINIA:
Mrs. Woolf is not at home. She has gone to Capri. So has Mr.
Woolf. He is meeting her in Capri.

[*She answers the phone.*]

Oh, Lady Colefax, Sybil, but how lovely. Perhaps we could, let me
just ask.

[*She reaches over and whispers to* LEONARD.]

It's for Wednesday. Arnold Bennett, Max Beerbohm, George
Moore, Mr. Yeats.

[*He shakes his head to say no.*]

VIRGINIA [*into the phone*]:
We should love it. It's what I've wanted so much. I've been leading
the life of a badger. Yes, Wednesday.

[*She puts the phone down.*]

LEONARD:
You forget that on first meeting her she reminded you of the
cherries on a servant's hat.

VIRGINIA:
Now don't spout columns of fury at me. Be nice to Mandrill.

LEONARD:
Everything has to be rationed, work, and walking and people and parties.

VIRGINIA:
But you can't deny me my social side.

LEONARD:
I mind when they drain you.

VIRGINIA:
It's a trait I inherited from my mother—the joy of meeting people, being stimulated.

LEONARD:
And dissipated.

VIRGINIA:
Meeting people, taking the risk.

LEONARD:
Risks imply falls.

VIRGINIA:
If we don't live venturously what is the point? We are like the most common animated little slugs.

[*They talk rapidly and excitedly.*]

On July the first the Woolfs had Philip and Irene Noel-Baker to tea . . .

LEONARD:
And dined out.

VIRGINIA:
On the second Lytton's sister Dorothy Bussy came to tea.

LEONARD:
On the third Raymond Mortimer and Hope Mirrlees dined at Tavistock Square.

VIRGINIA:
On July the fifth . . .

LEONARD:
Sunday . . .

VIRGINIA:
We went to a performance of *The Rehearsal.*

LEONARD:
On the sixth Virginia dined with Clive.

VIRGINIA:
Just to rub up my wits. On the ninth . . .

LEONARD:
George Rylands . . .

VIRGINIA:
Came to tea.

LEONARD:
T. S. Eliot after dinner.

VIRGINIA:
Pale marmoreal Tom.

LEONARD:
By midsummer the soirées and the worldly life dogged us.

VIRGINIA:
Into the drawing room, which was full, bright, miscellaneous. If one's normal pulse is seventy, then in five minutes it was one hundred and twenty. And the blood not the sticky, white fluid of daytime but brilliant and prickly like champagne.

Scene Five

VIRGINIA:
Shakespeare would have liked us tonight. Full of brio. I'm glad Clive minced that little man, that little weasely man. I thought he said the Holy Ghost whereas in fact he said the whole coast. . . . So I said, "The Holy Ghost . . . where is the Holy Ghost?" and he said, "Wherever the sea is." Am I mad, I thought, or is this wit? . . . "The Holy Ghost?" I said. . . . "No," he said, "the whole coast."

LEONARD:
I could have done without Mr. Yeats's disquisition on Fairies.

VIRGINIA:
And you held up the proceedings of the soup with your fidgets.

LEONARD:
I was thinking up scientific forms of suicide for most of them there.

VIRGINIA:
Particularly Mr. Arnold Bennett.

LEONARD:
He said, "W . . . Woolf does n . . . not like my n . . . novels."

VIRGINIA:
Oh, but you did fidget; you were like this.

LEONARD:
I came perilously close to ruining a tablecloth.

VIRGINIA:
Stephen Tomlin is fleeing like Daphne from lovers, fleeing to where no one shall follow him. He's half crazy, wishing to love and to

give, and finding—and this appalls him—that people love him in return. No one returns mine.

[*She nudges him. She is trying to get from him a reaction, a joke.*]

You liked Miss Gertrude Stein, you got on with her, throned on her broken seat. All of Edith Sitwell's furniture is derelict, so to make up for that she is stuck about with jewels. Miss Stein, the swathed sausage, thinks *she* is the most intelligible and also the most popular writer in the world—"A rose is a rose is a rose." Is it? Despises people of English birth; come to think of it, so do I. The charm of the young Englishwoman eludes me. Eyes like dogs and great plaits down their backs, and what, pray, did you make of Mrs. Nicolson, Miss Vita Sackville, mother, wife, great lady, hostess, and scribbler.

LEONARD:
I didn't talk to her.

VIRGINIA:
No need. She has a weak chin. I don't like women with mustaches. She's like an overripe grape. She writes twenty thousand words in a fortnight. She's a factory. An ancestor of theirs took the death warrant to Mary Stuart, and so touched was she by the delicacy of his approach that she gave him a prayer book as a present. It's in the private chapel at Knole, the family seat.

LEONARD:
She is about to be disinherited and her mother's mad.

VIRGINIA:
Just like you to get the facts.

[*He hands her a glass of milk but* VIRGINIA *disdains it.*]

Oh no, not milk and rest, not all that again.

[*She knocks on the table.*]

Must, must, must, must sleep, must rest, no dining out, no galli-
vanting. Alone in my burrow.

[*He puts the milk a distance away.*]

Don't fuss me. Don't coop me up.

What I think of is arriving and seeing Vita black and scarlet under
a lamp. The garden full of lust and bees.

Equanimity, Mrs. Woolf, practice equanimity.

I shall be cold, I shall be hostile, I shall be indifferent.

Mrs. Nicolson.

[*She smiles.*]

The Hon. Mrs. Nicolson. Snob that I am, I trace your passions five
hundred years back and they become romantic to me. I have a
perfectly untrue but romantic vision of you in my mind, stamping
out the hops in a great vat in Kent, stark naked . . . [*she laughs*]
brown as a satyr and very beautiful. How long do you take to milk
on your great estate and how do you cool it and do you churn and
make butter? Facts, Mrs. Nicolson, facts.

[*To* VITA] You do, I suppose, disapprove of my dress, my apparel.

VITA:
It's dreadful.

VIRGINIA:
I was advised by the Editor of *Vogue,* a Mrs. Todd, to wear this.
It cost me four guineas, and look at my gloves.

[*She is* not *wearing gloves.*]

VITA:
Todd! So you whore after *her.*

VIRGINIA:
Better whore after her than timidly copulate with the Editor of the
Times Literary Supplement.

VITA:
So long as one goes the whole hog.

VIRGINIA:
Oh, Mrs. Nicolson . . . Do you cut up rough, like a baroness?

VITA:
I would say not as rough as you. You see people, but you don't feel
them. . . . We, they, are all material to you.

VIRGINIA:
In that case let's stick to literature; it's simpler. For instance, one
test of poetry is that without saying things, indeed saying the
opposite, it conveys things. I read Crabbe and I think of fens,
marshes, shingle, rivers. . . . But there is nothing of the sort. There
is how Lucy got engaged to Edward Shore.

VITA:
You should wear shorter skirts and show off your shins.

VIRGINIA:
They are not my best point.

VITA:
Captious, aren't you?

VIRGINIA:
And you, what are you?

VITA:
A woman—yes, but a million other things. A snob? Ancestors—
proud of them. Greedy, luxurious, vicious, don't care a damn. Like
lying in bed on fine linen listening to the pigeons.

VIRGINIA:
Like giving pain.

VITA:
Silver, victuals, wine, maids, footmen, spoiled perhaps.

VIRGINIA:
You are so much in full sail, on the high tide.

VITA:
When shall I take you there?

VIRGINIA:
Where?

VITA:
Home, to Long Barn.

VIRGINIA:
I shall see a table laid with jugs of chocolate and buns.

VITA:
You shall sit beneath the arras, you shall eat game, and there will
be fireworks down by the frozen pond.

VIRGINIA [*marveling*]:
Ottoline took me motoring one night here in London and the effect
was stupendous—St. Paul's, Tower Bridge, moonlight, the river.
Ottoline in full dress and paint, white and gaudy like a tombstone,
all the hoppers and bargees coming home drunk. It was the Bank
Holiday. Sometimes London can be very vivid. I was on the top
of a bus going to Waterloo, and there was an old beggar woman,
blind, in Kingsway, holding a mongrel in her arms and singing.
There was a recklessness about her.

VITA:
Just say when.

VIRGINIA [*to the Audience*]:
I am not sure that I am not throwing myself overboard.

VITA [*very sportingly*]:
What used we young fellows in the cockpit of the *Marie Rose* to
say about a woman who threw herself overboard? Ah, we had a
word for her.

VIRGINIA:
Ah, we must omit that word; it is disrespectful in the extreme.

VITA:
Shall we say Tuesday?

VIRGINIA:
I shall let Leonard decide that.

[*To* LEONARD] I am growing old and want more mustard with my
meat.

[VITA *and* VIRGINIA *come downstage.*]

I'm crack-brained . . . sometimes I am not Virginia at all.

VITA:
And now?

VIRGINIA:
Now I am a little drunk . . . this wine, for instance, I see it as amber
. . . and the beams are swaying and it's bliss, and I find you one
of the nicest and most magnanimous of women.

VITA:
Catch.

VIRGINIA:
You say you esteem me. That's damn cold. Still, I accept it like the
humble servant I am.

[*Aside*]

She has found me, she has kissed me, all is shattered.

VITA:
Good God, you are not going to give me chastity. The whole edifice
of female government and wiliness is based on that foundation
stone. Women are not chaste.

VIRGINIA:
Do you know that from your husband?

VITA:
I know it from my experience as a man.

VIRGINIA:
Were you?

VITA:
Yes.

[*Like a knight, she falls on one knee and speaks in a cavalier voice.*]

Falling on his knees, the Archduke Harry made the most passion-
ate declaration of his suit. He told her that he had something like
twenty million ducats in a strongbox at his castle. He had more
acres than any nobleman in England. The shooting was excellent.
He could promise her a mixed bag of ptarmigan and grouse such
as no English moor or Scottish either could rival. True, the pheas-
ants had suffered from the gape in his absence and the does had
slipped their young.

VIRGINIA [*in the same vein*]:
As he spoke, enormous tears formed in his violet eyes.

VITA [*unable to resist laughing*]:
But that don't count. Want to eat?

VIRGINIA:
Can't eat.

VITA:
A little of the fat, ma'am?

VIRGINIA:
Not yet, ma'am.

VITA:
Would you like to play Fly Loo?

VIRGINIA:
What is it?

VITA:
It's gambling. Great sums of money can be lost, and if you lose you will have to marry me.

VIRGINIA:
Show me.

VITA:
I bet you . . . that a fly will land on this lump of sugar. Now you choose your lump.

[VIRGINIA *hesitates and then points to one, and then they both look around expecting flies.* VITA *snaps her fingers impatiently.*]

VITA:
C'mon, flies, bluebottles, c'mon . . . don't be so sluggish.

VIRGINIA:
I expect they're asleep; it's winter.

VITA:
We'll change that.

[VITA *lets out a whistle as she dashes from one corner to another to try to arouse them.*]

VIRGINIA:
Life and a lover. It does not scan.

VITA [*acting voice*]:
Dammit, madam, you are loveliness incarnate.

VIRGINIA:
Trembled. Turned hot. Turned cold.

VITA [*still acting voice*]:
For she smiled the involuntary smile which women smile when their own beauty seems not their own.

Confronts them all of a sudden in a glass. And then she listened and heard only the leaves blowing and the sparrows twittering and then she sighed, life and a lover, it does not scan.

VIRGINIA:
Would you like to crack a man over the head and tell him he lies in his teeth?

VITA:
A pox on them, I say.

VIRGINIA:
And then she turned on her heel with extraordinary rapidity, whipped her emeralds from her neck.

VITA:
Stripped her satin from her back.

VIRGINIA:
Stood erect in her neat black silk knickerbockers and . . . (*does it*) rang the bell.

[*The bell or gong is heard to ring throughout the house. No one answers it.*]

VITA:
We are alone.

VIRGINIA:
Let us go.

Act Two

Scene One

[LEONARD WOOLF *is standing by the printing press, having something printed. The light in the room is candlelight. It is late afternoon in winter.*

VITA *enters. She is wearing a velvet jacket, a red striped skirt and an enormous, long rope of pink pearls. She is carrying a manuscript.*

LEONARD *greets her a little warily.*]

LEONARD:
It's thawing at last.

VITA:
Yes . . . drips everywhere.

LEONARD:
I'm afraid the gas has failed.

VITA [*mocking*]:
No hot baths!

[*She proffers him the manuscript.*]

It's my new poem, it's rather long. . . . Virginia said you might be interested. Not that I think she likes it. She says there is something in my writing that doesn't vibrate. She *is* devilish.

LEONARD:
She can be devilish. [*Pause*] She can be many things. She says her soft crevices are lined with hooks.

VITA:
How did you propose to Virginia?

LEONARD:
The usual way.

VITA:
And did she accept, in the usual way? Or did she . . . demur?

LEONARD:
First she said no. Then on the twenty-ninth of May I was having
lunch with her in her room when suddenly she told me that she
loved me and *would* marry me. We took a train to Maidenhead and
I hired a boat and rowed up the river to Marlow. Then we came
back and dined at a restaurant, a riverside restaurant. In all it was
ten hours. We seemed to drift through a beautiful vivid dream.

VITA:
I can just imagine it.

LEONARD:
Such moments are only moments; they pass in a flash. Before one
knows it one is again in and of the herd.

VITA:
I think she enjoyed her stay at Long Barn.

LEONARD [*coldly*]:
I'm sure she did. She says you lavish on her the maternal protection
that she most wishes from everyone.

VITA [*sharply*]:
So what is the danger then?

LEONARD:
She has to lead a quiet, almost vegetative life.

VITA:
She says to live venturously is the thing.

LEONARD:
You don't know her. She leaves the ground, she follows her voices. She stumbles after them.

VITA:
And what do they tell her?

LEONARD:
Everything. She goes through every stage. She goes beyond reach.

[*He points to a chaise longue.*] For the last three weeks she lay there in a whirlpool . . . temperature 101, 102.

VITA:
Are you asking me to give her up?

LEONARD:
I am telling you to be careful.

[VITA *laughs heartily.*]

VITA:
That's just what Harold says, he says it's smoking over a petrol tank.

LEONARD:
He's right.

VITA:
But she is an exquisite companion, vulnerable, sensitive, and, for the record, I do love her.

LEONARD:
Backstairs?

VITA:
It's a spiritual thing, an intellectual thing. She inspires a feeling of tenderness.

LEONARD:
Her terror is of going mad again.

VITA:
She has told me some of your life together . . . she was quite open
about it.

LEONARD:
You may think that you have guessed our secrets, but for each of
us there is something more, something deeper.

VITA:
As with me and Harold . . . for each of us the other is the magnetic
north. So let's not quibble over things.

[VIRGINIA *can be seen coming towards the door.*]

LEONARD:
It's not just playing with fire.

VITA:
Oh, but how satisfying if it loosens the lineaments.

VIRGINIA:
Ah, Vita . . . the sovereign. [*She smiles, surprised.*] I've been to the
dentist again. My cheek is all blistered from having a tooth
stopped. I say to him, "Why do you do this to me?" and he says,
"But then, Mrs. Woolf, your skin is the most sensitive in all Lon-
don."

[*Feeling her skin*] At which I am flattered. Leonard paints my skin
with zinc ointment, which I lick. I daresay it's poisonous and I
shall be dead.

[*Turning to the cluttered table*] Shall we have tea?

LEONARD:
I've got to go to Hampstead to a meeting.

VIRGINIA [*sarcastically*]:
Oh, what is to be the big subject today—the Dyestuff Bill, the thyroid gland, the freedom of the marriage couch?

[*To* VITA] His secretary is like a chest of drawers, and his mother, Mrs. Woolf Senior, keeps a basket of undarned socks next to her bed so that when she wakens she can darn them straight away. That's where Leonard got his application.

LEONARD [*to* VITA]:
Virginia is at her best when she is in wrath.

[LEONARD *goes out.* VIRGINIA *is standing by the lace curtain and she clings to it for a moment while she and* VITA *look at each other, manifesting shyness and desire.*]

VIRGINIA [*tentatively*]:
Well.

VITA:
Well.

VIRGINIA:
I left a nightgown behind and a grisly powder puff.

VITA:
Buffles has sent them on. . . . Was quite impressed with you . . . he'd seen your photo in *The Listener.*

VIRGINIA:
Does he ever catch you in the act?

VITA:
No.

VIRGINIA:
Your husband wrote to me.

VITA:
Yes, he said he would.

VIRGINIA [*reading*]:
"I am glad that Vita has come under an influence so stimulating and so sane.

[*She lets out a hoot of laughter.*]

"You need never worry about my having any feelings except a longing that Vita's life should be as rich and as sincere as possible. I loathe jealousy as I loathe all forms of disease."

VITA:
You and I must be the two happiest married women in all of London.

VIRGINIA:
But the soul is by nature unmated, is it not?

VITA:
You look ravishing.

VIRGINIA:
I feel like some dowdy decrepit horrible dingy old fly.

VITA [*coyly*]:
Fishing, are you?

VIRGINIA:
Come to demoralize me?

VITA:
Yes, darling, to haunt your terrace.

VIRGINIA:
Isn't it like living in a damp dustbin?

VITA:
Yes, a bit commonplace but good for the chastity.

VIRGINIA:
Bad Vita. Bad wicked Vita.

[VIRGINIA *draws the lace curtain across the center of the stage.* VITA *comes and stands next to her.* VIRGINIA *starts to knot the pearl necklace into great eggs.*]

VITA:
I was worried stiff about you . . . all that fever.

VIRGINIA:
And burning desire.

VITA:
What did they say was wrong?

VIRGINIA:
Everything was put down to you . . . seeing you, much too rackety.

VITA:
You told them!

VIRGINIA:
No, they guessed. People always guess one's innermost secrets. They gave me stiff doses of bromide. . . . It's rather nice, one floats like a log. I would waken only to write to you or to read your letters. You can't imagine what it meant to me to see your blue envelope, to open it, and to find the second letter hidden inside the "proper" one. . . .

VITA [*excited voice*]:
You know what I wanted to do . . . steal my motorcar out of the garage, come here at night, throw gravel at your window . . . you'd come down and let me in and I'd stay till five.

VIRGINIA:
Rake.

VITA:
Enchantress.

VIRGINIA:
Yours is the only face I have in my mind's eye, and if I may be so coarse, your legs, too, like beech trees.

[VITA *backs away from* VIRGINIA.]

VITA:
And I'm here now under your merciless eye.

VIRGINIA:
Have you yielded to someone else, some wench, some pantry maid?

VITA:
No.

VIRGINIA:
Please be honest with me.

[VITA *smiles and then in a whisper resorts to pet names.*]

VITA:
Potto . . . Bosman . . . Weevil.

[VIRGINIA *is both reassured and melted by this intimacy.*]

VIRGINIA:
Feel my heart.

[VIRGINIA *crosses to allow* VITA *to feel her heart.*]

VIRGINIA:
The doctor came every day and took out a little silver stethoscope

and said there was nothing wrong with it . . . but there is, there is.

VITA:
It's going wild, it's like a young bucking mare.

VIRGINIA:
Kiss me.

[*They kiss. It is a long impassioned kiss.* VITA *is the first to break the embrace. She opens the top buttons of her blouse and from her bodice takes out a bunch of snowdrops. She hands them to* VIRGINIA.]

VIRGINIA:
The first snowdrops.

VITA:
The very first.

VIRGINIA:
Oughtn't you send them to Harold?

[*Pause.*]

VITA:
I shall be seeing him . . . I shall be joining him in Persia. . . . I came to say au revoir.

[VIRGINIA *turns away, stunned.*]

VIRGINIA:
So you have the wanderlust again.

VITA:
To see my husband, yes.

VIRGINIA:
I have no time for people in ambassadorial states . . . a lot of
humbug and falseness.

VITA:
I have no time for them either.

VIRGINIA [*anxiously*]:
When do you go?

VITA [*conciliatory*]:
Don't take it badly.

VIRGINIA:
Of course not; we gain as much as we lose by this sort of thing.
[*Getting angrier.*] Sure, chuck me, why not, you simply tacked me
onto your equipage for a time.

VITA:
It's not my doing . . . it's life.

VIRGINIA [*almost to herself*]:
Dismal. Dismal.

[VITA *goes to her now to try and reassure her.*]

VITA:
Your mind so hard and yet you are a child. You are afraid.

VIRGINIA:
So many brilliant schemes came into my head . . . rendezvous,
scenes, solutions . . . now extinguished.

VITA:
It is bloody . . . in fact, I don't know if I can tear myself away.

VIRGINIA [*vehemently*]:
Go. Go.

[VITA *looks at her for a moment, sees how adamant she is and goes.*]

[VIRGINIA *is holding the bunch of snowdrops and now starts to walk, or, rather, to stalk around the stage—this is a particular characteristic of hers and happens when she is agitated. During her walk-talk she tears the snowdrops.*]

VIRGINIA:
"Parting," as the poet says, "would turn our hearts into clocks. . . ." I suppose I could read Doris Dalglish and see what it's like to have nerves and live in Wandsworth with one's mother.

Gone and left me in a pucker.

Now you are arriving, driving into the gates of Teheran. There's Harold coming out to meet you. There you sit proud as a peacock. Now you are stopping at some place for figs and wine, you are very excited, all in a whirl, like a flock of birds flying about. Yes, you are an agile animal—no doubt about it . . . heart you have none.

Harold is a happy man and I am an envious woman. I cannot hold out hopes that you are thinking of me.

By the way, Leonard thinks your dog is a hermaphrodite. I didn't tell you but we went to Violet Bonham Carter's last night, or did I? Philip Ritchie told me I was the chief coquette in London; no, "Allumeuse," Clive corrected him. [*In sharper tone*] Allumeuse.

Then my suspenders came down, dragging with them an old rag of chemise—why didn't you tell me one must fasten one's suspenders properly? Always some misery like suspenders to clip my wings of glory. I played a little trick. I had no hat. Bought one for seven shillings and eleven pence at a shop in Oxford Street: green felt, the wrong colored ribbon; all a-flop like a pancake in midair. Even I thought it looked odd. But I wanted to see what happens among real women if one of them looks like a pancake in midair. In came the dashing vermeil-tinctured Mrs. Edwin Montagu. She started. She deplored me. Then hid a smile. Looked again. Thought, ah, what a tragedy. Liked me even as she pitied. Overheard my flirting. Was puzzled. Finally conquered. You see, women can't hold out against this kind of flagrant disavowal of womanliness . . . they open their arms as to a bird in a blast.

How are you? Any malaria? I'm so solitary . . . my brain a whirligig, in bed at night, as I walk the streets, everywhere, in the lamplight, you in your emeralds . . .

We are still here talking about love and sodomy. Morgan Forster says he's worked it out and one spends three hours on food, six on sleep, four on work, two on love. Lytton says ten on love. I say the whole day on love. I say it's seeing things through a purple shade. "But you've never been in love," they say.

Damned lustrous face of yours. I wish to God I'd asked you to wire.

VIRGINIA [*reading letter*]:
Come to Greece. Join us there. I leave it to your imagination to guess what it would mean to me if I saw you coming down the gangplank.

What would it mean to you if you saw me coming down the gangplank? What would it mean to me?

[*Harsher voice*] What would happen if I let myself over a precipice —marked V? No, I won't come. I shall stay here and write about it. That shall be my victory. Ain't people cussed?

Orlando. A Biography.

Stuck a pair of pistols in her belt, finally wound about her person several strings of emeralds and pearls of the finest orient which had formed part of the ambassadorial wardrobe.

LEONARD:
For women are not obedient, chaste-scented and exquisitely appareled by nature. They can only attain these graces, without which they may enjoy one of the delights of life, by the most serious discipline.

VIRGINIA:
This done she leaned out of the window, gave one low whistle and descended the shattered and bloodstained staircase. . . .

LEONARD:
There in the shadow of a giant fig tree waited an old gypsy on a donkey. He led another by the bridle. Orlando swung her leg over it and thus attended by a lead dog, riding a donkey in the company of a gypsy, left Constantinople.

VIRGINIA:
They rode for several days and nights and met with a variety of adventures. . . .

LEONARD:
Some at the hands of men, some at the hands of nature.

VIRGINIA:
Is it bad? Is it rubbish? Is it slovenly?

LEONARD:
It's different—it's spry.

VIRGINIA:
I began it as a joke.

LEONARD:
It will keep them guessing.

VIRGINIA [*tenderly*]:
The consequence of not always being with one's husband is that one begins to talk and write nonsense.

LEONARD:
I predict that it will sell.

VIRGINIA:
And we shall buy a house in the country and put down a pair of trees. What I like about the country is that I can read there. So divine to come in from a walk to have tea by the fire and read and read, say *Othello*, say anything.

LEONARD:

But even if Shakespeare or Montaigne should knock on the door we shall pretend to be out.

VIRGINIA:

You see I would not have married you had I not preferred living with you to anyone else.

[LEONARD *picks up a small diary, reads it and laughs.*]

LEONARD:

Do you want to hear what our factotum office boy is saying about us? [*Quoting*] *Orlando* is selling like hot cakes. LW, Svengali, is terrified we will run out of stock and it's my job to count the copies and put them into packages. Mrs. W. has bought a very smart winter outfit, long, Russian style, black, cossack coat of astrakhan and a Russian hat.

VIRGINIA:

Coins in my pocket, how luxurious. Soon I shall be as well paid as a Civil Servant.

LEONARD:

How would you like to be picked up out of here and set down in one of the wildest moors in England to see the eclipse?

VIRGINIA:

Wrapped in a blanket?

LEONARD:

The sun sails at a furious pace and the next moment it's gone behind clouds.

VIRGINIA:

Is that all?

LEONARD:

No . . . for twenty-four seconds a sudden plunge, into darkness.

VIRGINIA:
How does the light return to the world?

LEONARD:
Miraculously, then normally, always with a great sense of relief.

Scene Two

[LEONARD *is gardening.* VIRGINIA *comes out. She is edgy. Bird song.*]

VIRGINIA:
A nightingale?

LEONARD:
No . . . a daybird.

VIRGINIA:
What are you planting?

LEONARD:
Iris.

[VIRGINIA *looks up at the birds.*]

VIRGINIA:
Syllabling away, discordantly . . . Life . . . life . . . I stayed up too late.

LEONARD:
Everyone liked your play.

VIRGINIA:
Brightwater—a farce. I should have taken my bow on a donkey.

LEONARD:
The children loved it. They loved the tribes of elves and the baying ape.

VIRGINIA:

Who was that elderly virgin Clive brought—with stationary eyes like an oyster?

LEONARD:

A Miss Buchanan. She's from Cheltenham.

VIRGINIA:

Women like her have no reason to exist, in this world or in the next.

LEONARD:

Maynard is back from America. He says it is an impossible climate . . . it has collected all the faults of all the climates and nobody could produce a great work there.

VIRGINIA:

Because of the climate! He says I live and write in an opium dream.

LEONARD:

Old Maynard. The doughty defier of God. Quite stingy, he and Lydia; two grouse for eleven people.

VIRGINIA:

I left my shawl at Nessa's. I always leave something; and I cry— I don't know why, I cry. She shuts me out, oh, yes, she does. . . . She detests emotion. Her children drew us apart. Yet I do love them. You see, I am undependable.

LEONARD:

Did I tell you I met George Bernard Shaw the other day in Longacre—he said he was inspired to write *Heartbreak House* when he first met you.

VIRGINIA:

He doesn't like me, he doesn't like what I write—too vapid, not practical enough and not partial. Wyndham Lewis doesn't like me either . . . or Mr. Cyril Connolly.

LEONARD:
That is just the usual litter of undergraduate venom.

VIRGINIA [*sharply*]:
"I am a peeper not a looker. I am fundamentally a prude." There
is a queer disreputable pleasure in being abused, in being a martyr.
I shall write a pamphlet On Being Despised.

LEONARD:
They cannot touch you; only as a pebble skims the shore.

VIRGINIA:
I don't understand history—well, maybe I don't. I am an outsider.
I experiment with my imagination. . . . The pack may howl but it
shall never catch me.

LEONARD:
Such violent feelings.

VIRGINIA:
You'd like to save the world from its follies . . . well it can't be done.
Men think it can . . . with their cold, weathertight, admirable,
caustic, laconic, objective imaginations. All that boring, blearing
politics.

LEONARD:
Look . . . we'll have lots of pears, the tree is swagged with fruit.

VIRGINIA:
I should have had children, Leonard. I should have had. I am
angry with myself for not having taken the risk. Carrington bears
none of Ralph's children, nor Alix any of James's, nor Frances—
ain't it odd how all the flowers of female youth and spent youth
will die with their buds unopened.

LEONARD:
You have nephews, nieces, oodles of friends; you say if I meet one
more person I will pullulate.

VIRGINIA [*softly*]:
You were afraid for me, weren't you?

LEONARD:
It is not a world for children any more. The die is cast. It is now a question, an impending question, of war versus peace, ugliness versus beauty, civilization versus savagery.

VIRGINIA:
Leonard, have you never wanted a Lavinia or a Jane or a Geraldine or a Penelope?

LEONARD:
No, only a Virginia.

VIRGINIA:
Grey as a scullery pail and her hair falls in the soup.

LEONARD:
And she writes in the mold of eternity.

VIRGINIA:
Nonsense. Crumbs, Variations, Possibilities, Bad shots.

LEONARD:
Supple, naked and always to the truth.

VIRGINIA:
And you?

LEONARD:
Too much facts, too hidebound.

VIRGINIA:
I cried when you made your speech at the Labour Party Conference. Mr. Bevin's attack on Lansbury was dramatic but too vitriolic, too grasping.

LEONARD:
I thought I was a bit artificial . . . the battered man hawking his conscience about.

VIRGINIA:
Do you think that?

LEONARD:
I think that we like carrying our private cross.

[LEONARD *goes toward the exit.*]

VIRGINIA:
Where are you going?

LEONARD:
Someone's come.

VIRGINIA:
Maybe it's Nessa, bringing back my shawl. I hope it is. . . . I shall have to tell her. . . . How I distrust the maternal instinct—it is immeasurable and unscrupulous and destructive and limiting.

LEONARD [*as he goes*]:
You did stay up too late.

VIRGINIA:
I have sucked so much of your time and your sap.

[LEONARD *comes back in.*]

LEONARD:
It's a journalist.

VIRGINIA:
A what?

LEONARD:
He says you made an appointment, he rang earlier.

VIRGINIA:
I thought it was the vet about the cow's sciatica. I can't. I won't.
I will not rub my face in that pail of offal.

[VIRGINIA *runs toward a corner of the room in fear.* LEONARD *goes out.*]

VIRGINIA:
He'd come in here and get his little notebook out and cross his legs
and say, "Mrs. Woolf, you have been credited as a feminist and
hinted at as a sapphist; what do you feel about that?" [*Pretending
to reply.*] Oh, yes . . . women owe a great deal to me. . . . I have
been for women, in my way. . . . I have told them not to be looking
glasses to their menfolk. [*Long pause.*] "Mrs. Woolf, it is said that
you have remolded the English language. How do you feel about
that and how do you cope with the celebrity business?" I don't
know. I am an elderly, dowdy, fussy, ugly, incompetent woman.
I am tired. I can make bread. I invent menus.

[*Confessional voice*] Gradually he would winkle it out of me—up
at eight, wash, breakfast, out to my garden shed for three hours.
Lunch at one, rissoles—or halibut—then custard, and a smoke,
then into thick shoes and take my dog Pinka on his lead and up
the hill to the shepherd's cottage, or the Piddinghoe farm, back
home along the river, tea at four, letter writing . . .

[*Stronger voice*] Queer, the contraction of life to a village radius.
Very small beer. In London now I'd be owling through the streets.
More pack and thrill than here. Our habits, our fluency, these
things you see me by, these are pretenses. . . . Beneath, it is all dark
and it is spreading. . . .

[LEONARD *comes in and she emerges from her hiding. He turns his
back on her. She sees that he is upset.*]

VIRGINIA:
In a huff . . . It's gloom for the day now . . . stony silence.

LEONARD:
Hitler has attacked Poland.

[VIRGINIA *lets out a cry.*]

LEONARD [*continuing*]:
And Danzig is to be incorporated into the Reich. . . . We are at war.

VIRGINIA:
We are?

LEONARD:
He just told me.

VIRGINIA:
What do we do now?

LEONARD:
Our lovely country destroyed. Our manor houses, our moats, our downs.

VIRGINIA:
Will they cross the Channel?

LEONARD:
Who knows? An insane underdog suddenly sees himself as all-powerful. . . . Bombs are falling in Warsaw now, and soon, they will be falling here.

VIRGINIA:
How is one killed by a bomb, I wonder—a swoon, a drum . . . two or three gulps attempting consciousness—and then, dot dot dot.

[*He turns to her.*]

LEONARD:
Don't, dearest, don't.

[*He walks toward her.*]

LEONARD [*calmly*]:
I am not afraid. [*Pause.*] We are not afraid.

One feels numbed, really. All the young men that will be smashed up.

[*Their irritation is now replaced by a solicitude, a tenderness created by the news of the greater horror.* VIRGINIA *looks at him solicitously.*]

VIRGINIA:
If the Germans cross the Channel you might have to wear a yellow star . . . or, they might take you away . . .

LEONARD:
No [*gravely*], if it comes to that, we will gas ourselves, in our garage.

VIRGINIA:
We will never be parted?

LEONARD:
Never.

[LEONARD *puts an arm around her.*]

VIRGINIA:
Oh, it is such an enormous thing being wanted . . . a wife.

LEONARD [*quoting*]:
"Look thy last on all things lovely . . . every hour."

VIRGINIA:
I am not beautiful, any more.

LEONARD:
Oh, but you are . . . you are.

[*They kiss in a tender, platonic way.*]

Scene Three

[*Six months later.*]

[VIRGINIA'S *voice is heard offstage.*]

VIRGINIA:
No books published.

No public.

No audience.

No echo.

[*She comes onstage, which is in semidarkness.*]

That's part of one's death . . . and stinting on paper and sugar and butter and buying little hoards of matches to have . . .

[*During this speech she has lit the lamp. In the light of the lamp we now see that she is wearing a trenchcoat. She's wet; her hair is also completely wet. She takes off the trenchcoat then looks around as if to get her bearings.*]

VIRGINIA:
I begin now to forget, I begin to doubt the fixity of tables, the reality of here and now, to tap my knuckles smartly upon the edges of solid objects and say, "Are you hard?" I have been so many different things, have made so many different sentences, all lost in the process of eating and drinking. "Who am I?"

I was crossing the stream when . . .

The stream at the bottom of the garden where our wood meets the Black Wood.

Must prepare dinner. Fish forgotten . . . so what shall it be?
. . . Tripe and onions.

It's heavenly here. L and I alone.

[*She picks up a rug.*] And all the clothes-drudgery and all the social
drudgery obliterated. I will never dine with Lady Dilke again or
give a prize to a Frenchwoman. I went to London yesterday.

[*She puts the rug over her shoulder. Sadder voice*] All my old
squares gashed, dismantled, the red bricks all white powder, like
a builder's yard.

[*Braver voice*] I said to my horses "Home, John." My cohorts will
see me through.

What cohorts, Virginia, what cohorts? Is that you Leonard, is that
you?

Can't be you yet. Maybe it's Nessa. Is that you, Nessa?

The downs were like lions today . . . couchant . . . yellow, unstained
. . . you could paint them.

Nessa, don't shut me out. Don't say "Virginia lives in a world of
her own"; Virginia wants you here now, you and Leonard, the two
people I love most.

Brilliant amorous day was divided as sheerly from the night as land
from water. How tired I am of stories . . . how tired I am of phrases
that come down beautifully with their feet on the ground and die
like stars.

Nessa, I need you. Vita, I need you. Tell me you are soon coming.
I want to sink into your arms, to feel the festival and the firelight.

Dinner, halibut. You're late, Leonard. No trains, no cars, no pet-
rol, no butter. All our friends isolated over winter fires or in the
bomb sites.

[*To the Audience*] Yes, London was full of queues, children and
women, queueing for the air-raid shelter with their bags and their
blankets. Carpets nailed to windows, ceilings down, rubble.

Eight of my city churches destroyed, and the Guild Hall.

[*Suddenly thoughtful and in a sharper voice*] Leonard, why aren't you back? Perhaps you're . . . No, you're not; they don't raid till night and our private luck has not run out.

Leave me. I did nothing to deserve you . . . nothing. . . . Far from it.

[*She points to the window and beyond.*]

Our luck has not turned. Our pear tree is bearing fruit and I am a red admiral feasting on an apple.

And I am filling my mind with the Elizabethans—"Hang there like fruit my soul until the tree doth die." Who will be killed tonight? . . . not us, I say.

Dawn is some sort of whitening of the sky, some sort of renewal, another day, another Friday, another 20th March. . . . I'm not responsible for the world, I am *not* responsible.

[LEONARD *enters.*]

Ah, there you are, just in time. . . . I have dinner ready. A moment of great household triumph. Yes, I am a little triumphant.

LEONARD:
Are you wet?

VIRGINIA:
I slipped and fell in a ditch.

LEONARD:
Who were you talking to just now?

VIRGINIA:
You know me, tongue always clacking.

LEONARD:
But not so fast.

VIRGINIA [*rapidly*]:
A new book pumping in the brain. My mind is agape and red-hot
with it. It's in here [*taps her head*], stored. I shall scrape the sea
bed, clean.

Those are mine.

LEONARD:
Our house was bombed, the whole square was bombed last night.

VIRGINIA:
Funny that I didn't know, that I didn't guess.

LEONARD:
It's still smoldering. Miss P. salvaged what she could. She was in
overalls sweeping up everything. She didn't want you to be upset.

VIRGINIA:
And the press?

LEONARD:
It's damaged but it's not ruined. We're going to move to Letch-
worth tomorrow.

VIRGINIA:
Is the house completely gone?

LEONARD:
Yes. Just a great pile of brick and glass everywhere.

[*As he hands them to her*] I brought your diaries.

VIRGINIA [*on a happy note*]:
I feel quite exhilarated really at losing everything. It's like starting
again, quite bare.

[*Reading*] "A tree pelted with starlings." Pillicock sat on Pillicock's hill. Hark, hark. The dogs do bark.

LEONARD [*worried*]:
Virginia?

VIRGINIA [*very rapidly*]:
No, not leaving the ground, not this time, staying with feet on the ground.

LEONARD:
Shouldn't we see a doctor? You like our new doctor.

But you like Octavia; she's our friend.

VIRGINIA:
There's nothing the matter with me.

[*Pouting like a child*] She'll order a rest cure; I'll be sent away from Mongoose.

LEONARD:
Only if it's necessary.

VIRGINIA [*firmly*]:
It's not necessary. It's nothing. You were late. I was worried. Paralyzed. It was all so silent here.

LEONARD:
I'm sorry. There was a bomb scare at Richmond, and we all got out, then we went to Croydon; there was a siren there, we all got out, we had to wait for the all clear.

[*Humorously*] I couldn't find a public lavatory.

VIRGINIA [*wistfully*]:
"Then above the little grave we kissed again with tears."

LEONARD:
Virginia, are you sure?

VIRGINIA:
Yes, quite sure. I've got to start again on a book. This one has to be damned deep, the deepest of my adventures. No babble. No glibness. Something new in my pot . . .

We had our own little drama here today. [*Joyous voice*] The river burst its banks.

LEONARD:
I saw it, walking home. It's like the sea . . . it's white and misty.

VIRGINIA:
Dear old nature kicking her heels up.

LEONARD:
It even smelt like the sea.

VIRGINIA:
So my marsh walk is gone.

LEONARD:
Only for a day or so, until they mend the bank.

VIRGINIA:
The haystacks were in flood . . . sailing about . . . like the toy boats in Hyde Park so long ago . . . the water roaring through the gap in the hill. Poor Londoners with another night to face. Oh, the freedom . . . of here.

LEONARD:
I won't go up tomorrow.

VIRGINIA:
Oh, yes, you will. You see, I like my Mongoose going and I can think of him doing all the things he has to do, seeing to the move

of the press, talking to Miss P. . . . and getting me some books from the London Library.

LEONARD:
You would say if you were jangled.

VIRGINIA:
I have never been so well. You see the old hunger for books is on me, the childish passion, so that I am very "happy," as the saying is. Leonard, let us walk in the moonlight and see our own inland sea. We can walk along the edge and work up an appetite.

LEONARD [*taking her arm*]:
And if a raid comes a haystack is a very good thing to hide behind.

Scene Four

[*The country.*]

VIRGINIA:
And in me too the wave rises. It swells, it arches its back, it is death. . . .

My hair flying back like a young man's, like Percival's.

Against you I will fling myself unvanquished and unyielding . . . oh, death.

LEONARD:
Virginia!

[*Reading*]

Dearest,
I feel certain I am going mad again: I feel we cant go through another of those terrible times. And I shant recover this time. I begin to hear voices, and cant concentrate. So I am doing what seems the best thing to do. . . .

VIRGINIA:
You have been in every way all that anyone could be. I dont think two people could have been happier till this terrible disease came. I cant fight it any longer. If anybody could have saved me it would have been you. Everything has gone from me.

LEONARD:
We did not find her body for two weeks. Some children found her washed up near Lewes. There were heavy stones in the pocket of her jacket; it was terrible, it was the most terrible thing.

VIRGINIA:

I leant over the edge of the boat and fell down. I went under the sea. I have been dead and yet am now alive again—

[*Her voice gets quicker and quicker.*] and as before waking, the voices of the birds and the sound of wheels chime and chatter in a queer harmony, grow louder and louder, and the sleeper feels himself drawing towards the shores of life, the sun growing hotter, cries sounding louder, something tremendous about to happen.